The
Moment*um*
List

The Moment*um* List

REDISCOVER YOUR ABILITY TO **DELIGHT IN TIME**, RATHER THAN BE **MASTERED BY IT**

✧✗✧✗✧✗✧✗✧✗✧

DR. STEPHEN V. PETERS

The Momentum List:
Rediscover Your Ability to Delight in Time, Rather than Be Mastered
by It

Book Cover: Pete Rodriguez, Pete Design Company
Framework Design and Illustrations: Pete Rodriguez, Pete Design Company
Editing: Dr. Heather Jackson, Heather Jackson Consulting
Photography: Jan Macha
Typesetting and Editorial Design: Hadley Hendrix

First Edition
Printed in the United States of America

Year of Publication: 2024

Library of Congress Cataloguing-in-Publication Data: 2024923437
ISBN: 979-8-9919195-1-7 (Paperback)
ISBN: 979-8-9919195-0-0 (eBook)
ISBN: 979-8-9919195-2-4 (Hardcover)
ISBN: 979-8-9919195-3-1 (Audio Book)

Acknowledgements

This book would not have come to life without the invaluable contributions of a few remarkable individuals. In the spirit of celebrating the momentum behind this project, I want to express my heartfelt gratitude to those who made it possible:

April: My wife, whose support and encouragement provided the space I needed to focus on this project. If you are looking to *Land on Purpose in* your life, brand, family, or mission, you'll want to take full advantage of her services. Connect with her at landingonpurpose.com.

Mary Mitchell: A colleague turned trusted friend, our serendipitous conversation about reclaiming our time sparked the idea for a podcast that shares my journey towards a life that finds delight in time, rather than be mastered by it.

Dr. Heather Jackson (drheatherjackson.com): My brilliant editor and consultant, whose partnership and guidance helped shepherd my vision into reality—from spontaneous text exchanges to thorough manuscript revisions.

Peter Rodriguez and **Pete Design Company** (petedesigncompany.com): For their outstanding branding and visuals that Impeccably capture the essence of resetting your life for momentum.

Hadley Hendrix (hadleyhendrix.com): My talented editorial designer, who ensured we were publication-ready.

What an incredible team! Thank you all!

Contents

✧ ✧ ✧ ✧ ✧ ✧ ✧ ✧ ✧ ✧ ✧

Introduction

✧ ✧ ✧ ✧ ✧ ✧ ✧ ✧ ✧ ✧ ✧

I'M NOT A GURU, I'M JUST SOMEONE LIKE YOU WHO APPRECIATES ORDER

I like order and structure. I always have, which is why, for years, I worked on projects that required me to go into hard places or take on complex roles. I like the challenge of helping to reset environments and reframe relationships where chaos is doing more damage than good. As you can imagine, I have gotten pretty good at knowing what actions to take in these situations, especially when it comes to the well-being of other people.

Like you, I've categorized things to help me understand the current realities and demands of what needs to get done. I've written down what needs to get done and checked them off as I go. I'm goal-oriented and action-oriented, and I like to see what I have accomplished. I am sure you are, too. However, I've found over time that checking things off my To-Do List only showed what I had accomplished and amplified what I had not—leaving me enormously anxious and dissatisfied. In short, my To-Do list was a constant reminder that I was not getting the things that mattered to me the most, done. In most instances, the check marks next to completed tasks and actions often served other people's needs and supported other people's ambitions. Mine, not so much. This was for me, compounding evidence that I was investing persistently in someone else's hopes, vision, and dreams while falling short in making progress toward my own. I wanted to see a similar commitment of the time and energy I was giving to others shift to a healthier dose of investment in myself. It was time for a change.

Strategies for making the perfect To-Do List exist everywhere and in different forms; however, this book is about more than making the ideal To-Do List. It is about identifying, prioritizing, and getting done, what's most important for us- that thing that feeds our mind, will, emotions, and goals. It is about establishing and investing in your momentum.

When we identify and execute what's important to us, we can develop momentum on multiple levels—personally, professionally, and relationally. This momentum, then, provides the physical, emotional, and cognitive energy you need to be a benefit to others. That's why you need a Momentum List!

It's pretty simple: your Momentum List is likely already buried amongst the actions you have mapped out in your mind, on paper, and even on some virtual project management platform. However, that's the problem; it's buried. If you are like most people who are overscheduled, overwhelmed, and over-paced, it's likely buried under other people's priorities—your son's soccer schedule, your daughter's competitive martial arts itinerary, the new partnership initiative you've been tasked to manage, and the wellness needs of an elderly parent. If this is your life, you are in the worst possible position to make a sustained high-level contribution in the areas that matter most because you have not taken care of yourself first. The Momentum List is not about giving you something else to do. It's about re-examining and resetting what you already do or have a vision for doing but have allowed other people's problems and priorities to get in the way. It's about liberating yourself from being owned by time to *finding joy in time*. It's about getting unstuck, unburied, reenergized, and refueled with small wins daily so you can be more effective in helping others experience wins without resenting the time you spend doing things for them. It's about gaining momentum. Your momentum!

In this resource, you'll learn what it means to have momentum, why it's important, what's been stopping you from gaining it, and how to reorder and reorient your time and talents to what matters. To top it off, since everybody needs more than just a good idea for how to get things done, we've provided you with simple, actionable visual models of what reordering your most life-giving priorities can look like so that getting them in motion is an accessible experience for almost anyone at any stage of life. Let's get started!

1

❖ ❖ ❖ ❖ ❖ ❖ ❖ ❖ ❖ ❖ ❖

SPARKS OF EXCITEMENT OR
SOURCE OF ANXIETY

The word momentum sparks both exuberance and anxiety. Exuberance because having momentum means we are finding our stride, winning, or making that long hoped-for comeback after experiencing the disappointment of a series of setbacks. On the other hand, the word momentum can also insight anxiety. Why? Well, for many, the frustration of not being able to "catch a break" from what feels like a lifetime of heartbreak strikes a cord, they are not willing to have their heartstrings play. For others the anxiety stems from feeling like the ability to gain much-needed traction on a goal or new reality they are hoping for requires more physical or emotional strength than they have the time, energy, or cognitive room to provide at the moment. Sometimes the mere thought of that goal, target, or fulfillment of that experience—pursuing it, or as they say, "going after it", is enough to send them into a temporary depression. Their mind becomes assaulted with all kinds of thoughts intended to shame them for not thinking about taking action sooner— let alone actually doing it.

Sometimes the mere thought of that goal, target, or fulfillment of that experience—pursuing it, or as they say, "going after it", is enough to send them into a temporary depression because their mind becomes assaulted with all kinds of thoughts intended to shame them for not thinking about taking action sooner—let alone actually doing it.

Whether it's feelings of excitement or exhaustion that come to mind when you think of what it means to establish and live with momentum, this simple fact remains unchanged. The job of momentum is to provide you with the series of thoughts and actions that keep you moving in the desired direction, but it's your job to create the environment and set the conditions that facilitate the traction momentum provides.

AN OUTKAST OF MOMENTUM

In 2003, the legendary and critically acclaimed hip hop duo OutKast made of Antwan André Patton aka "Big Boi" and André Lauren Benjamin, better known by his stage name André 3000 released their fifth studio album,

"The job of momentum is to provide you with the series of thoughts and actions that keep you moving in the desired direction, but it's your job to create the environment and set the conditions that facilitate the traction momentum provides."

Speakerboxxx/The Love Below. This double album went on to become their best-selling album and the best-selling rap album of all time, selling over 11 million copies, and earning diamond status by the Record Industry Association of America (RIAA). However, this expansive and boldly delivered southern offering to hip hop almost didn't happen.

During a 2020 interview with record label executive L.A. Reid, on the Questlove Supreme Podcast, L.A. Reid recounts the events that led to the release of this record-breaking album—

> "*The real story was, it was Big Boi's solo album, right. And it was complete. And it was done and I heard "I Like the Way You Move", so I felt confident that we had like a big single. And Andre called, cause they weren't working together. I mean, this is fairly common knowledge, I think. They weren't working together. And* André *called the office, "Reed, when you droppin' Big Boi's album?"*

> I gave him the date. He was like, "*Ummmm!!! (clearing his throat). So if I want to drop an album with that, how much time do I have?*" And I think I told him, "*You got three weeks. He was like, "Three weeks!!! . . . Ahhhh!!!*" And I just remember him saying, OK. And he hung up. I didn't know what he had recorded because he really wasn't talking about it at all. He wasn't talking about making a record. Big Boi was going solo. We had already done a photo shoot. We've picked a single. We've

put the date on the calendar. We were moving forward and then I get that call from André and then he said, "How much time do I have?" That was the first time I had an indication that he wanted to make an album. He had not talked about it at all . . .

All I remember is that on the night that we had to turn the album in for parts so we could manufacture, Andre had studios going everywhere. He had mastering going on. He had a couple of mix rooms going on. He had an ensemble of studios going to make the deadline. He was working his ass off.

I went to the studio to visit and heard some of the material, but he finished it and sat down and played it for me. I could not believe what I was hearing, man. He played me, "Hey Ya". And I was like, oh my God!"

And, I didn't try to go into like, "Okay. Yeah, this is a smush. That wasn't how I reacted. I was more blown away that, "You actually did this in three weeks?" And I felt like you must have had this. There's no way you did this in three weeks."

André Lauren Benjamin's (aka André 3000) experience exemplified the job of momentum at work in his life and art. Whether he had the bulk of the material for the album already done or was still in the weeds of developing its unique blend of stylistic vibes, there is no question there was still an over-whelming amount of work that needed to be accomplished if he was going to meet that three-week deadline.

André 3000's experience during this window of time was likely filled with both exuberance and anxiety—the excite-ment of delivering his new album, offering his singularity of voice and funkadelic sound to his current fans and new audiences coupled with the anxiety of meeting a deadline to which his only mechanism of control was the lengths he would go to ensure he met it. André 3000 leveraged both sets of emotions to create a stride in his actions which in real time likely felt like a synchronized, chaotic symphony of move-ment that led to the creation of the finished product, *The Love Below*—his half of the double album. It was the combi-nation of clear, specific decisions and actions that served his primary objective of completing the album—a series of moments with people, places, and resources he wrangled together as he reoriented his time and talents to build the momentum desperately needed to get the job done.

So, at this point, you may be asking, *"If the job of momen-tum is to provide you with the series of thoughts and actions that keep you moving in the desired direction, how do I create the environment and set the conditions that facilitate the traction in my life momentum provides?* To help us answer that question, let's talk about the origins of momentum.

"André Lauren Benjamin's (aka André 3000) experience exemplified the job of momentum at work in his life and art."

2

✧✧✧✧✧✧✧✧✧✧✧

MOMENTUM DEFINED |
A CONCISE OVERVIEW OF MOMENTUM

The concept of Momentum was first introduced by the French scientist, mathematician, and philosopher, René Descartes (1596–1650). Not Issac Newton. While Issac Newton expanded on the idea of discoveries of motion with the three laws of motion principles, he owes his foundational insights on the topic to René Descartes. René Descartes asserted that motion has two states—the state of motion and the state of rest. Each of these is an act of movement. His research in the area of physics led him to assert that motion requires movement from at least two entities: the main object itself and the object that is applying weight or pressure on that object [Blackwell, 1966; Fowler, n.d.] Essentially, for momentum to be created, one thing has to be thrusted into motion, so things in its sphere of influence are also forced to move. Michael Fowler PhD., Professor Emeritus at The University of Virginia, Department of Physics offers an easy-to-understand example of Descartes's assertions on motion:

> *"Descartes' idea is best understood by considering a simple example: think first about someone (weighing say 45 kg/99.2 lbs.) standing motionless on high quality (frictionless) rollerskates on a level smooth floor. A 5 kg/11lbs. medicine ball is thrown directly at her by some-one standing in front of her, and only a short distance away, so that we can take the ball's flight to be close to horizontal. She catches and holds it, and because of its impact begins to roll backwards." —Fowler, M. (n.d.)*

The woman on the roller skates who was standing still had the potential for movement as a result of force thrown in her direction, which caused the wheels on her roller skates to make traction. What a great picture this is of real life! Each of us is capable of making movement and gaining traction. The question is, Are we making progress toward the values and priorities that matter most to us, or are we simply react-ing to whatever is thrown our way, causing us to fall out of sync with those values and priorities?

René Descartes' notions on the conservation of momentum tell us that momentum looks to preserve itself. In other words, the movement or traction that an individual or system makes in a particular direction remains constant and continuous unless it is acted upon by an external force. That means there has to be a deliberate act to change the force and direction of momentum if we want to see changes that align with our best interest.

While Issac Newton's first two laws of motion align very closely with Descartes' first two laws of nature, Newton's innovation and extended research on the theories of motion led to what we know as Newton's third law of motion—"Whenever one object exerts a force on another object, the second object exerts an equal and opposite on the first." *(A literal translation from its Latin origin.) Or* put in more commonly used terms . . . "For every action, there is an equal and opposite reaction."

This is particularly important when establishing momentum because it affirms that in any activity or area of life where you are looking to develop a steady flow of motion, an equal measure of resistance will be experienced. This is why developing momentum can feel so hard. For example, while I worked to complete this chapter, my wife and I were tactically and persistently teaching our 1-year-old a version of the words, "please" and "thank you" to help his often frenzied frustration with not having what he wants the moment he sees it. Between brief fits of dramatic tantrums and fallouts that mirrored a far worse reaction than someone who has just lost all of their prized possessions in a California wildfire, I have had to regroup and refocus myself so I could get back on track to what productivity enthusiast, Cal Newport, calls, "deep work" (Newport, 2016)—the uninterrupted investment of time and emotional energy to the cognitively demanding task of writing this chapter. Getting back on track with what I was writing proved to be cognitively taxing and emotionally draining because that brief, normal life disruption had initiated a thrust of my energy and attention in a direction that was out of alignment with where I wanted my energy and attention to go.

Subtle and familiar interruptions are not problematic or problems per se, but they are experiences that can and will, from time to time, throw our original well-laid plan into a different direction or require an alternative strategy. Be it life with an emerging toddler, the implementation of a project plan that didn't launch as intended, or a critical staffing issue that caught me off guard and pulled me from another task into the important people development side of my work, these are just examples of how I have experienced the tension of resistance to momentum in my own life. I'm sure you could think of ways this resistance shows up in your life. It is normal, but it can be frustrating if you do not have a daily plan for tending to what matters to you most as a proactive strategy for navigating the unexpected. The lack of a daily plan will give the resistance permission to eat your momentum alive!

"Subtle and familiar interruptions are not problematic or problems per se, but they are experiences that can and will, from time to time, throw our original well-laid plan into a different direction or require an alternative strategy."

To be frank, most of the activity of life is hoping you don't achieve momentum. Life would prefer you just follow the flow of the tide in whichever direction it's headed, even if it does not serve your best interest—your articulated hopes, your clearly defined vision, and specific goals. This kind of unfocused, misdirecting and dare I say, bullying of our time by priorities not of our choosing has other culprits as well. Two of the most notable culprits are: 1) the growing trend of being overworked (the demand on the body) and 2) the over-stimulating pressures of work (the demand on the mind), all in service to other people's agenda and the expense of our own.

3

"Many of us have been taken hostage by a worldview that values long hours focused on other people's business as a source to living a more fulfilled life, but there is clear evidence to counter that misconception."

❖ ❖ ❖ ❖ ❖ ❖ ❖ ❖ ❖ ❖ ❖ ❖

MOMENTUM IN CRISIS | A GLOBAL PHENOMENON

BEING OVERWORKED |
THE OVERLOOKED PANDEMIC BEFORE THE PANDEMIC

Being overworked was a thing way before the acceleration of working from home during and after our most recent global pandemic—COVID-19. To give this recent pandemic era all the credit for this growing societal dysfunction would be unfair and undermine your intelligence. The truth is the pandemic of overworked employees, entrepreneurs, and CEOs has been a phenomenon we have been trying to tackle for decades. The World Health Organization and International Labour Organization had become so concerned about the role of long work hours on people's mental and physical well-being that they joined forces to uncover the impact of what by the year 2000 had become a common practice of workers abandoning the familiar 35 to 40 hour work week in exchange for one that averaged 55 hours a week. A deep analysis of over 2,324 cross-sectional surveys focused on the influence of long work hours revealed some profound findings. Collectively these surveys had been administered to over 488 million people across 194 countries between the years 2000 and 2016. All of whom had experienced working a minimum of 55 hours a week. The findings from this analysis revealed this elongated work schedule came with some significant health risks, including increased levels of heart disease and stroke by those who worked 55 or more hours a week with increased regularity. The findings from this analysis also revealed that an estimated 745,194 deaths were associated with this escalated amount of time given to work. This study also found that as a result of long work hours, an estimated 22 to 24 years of life had been lost due to ischemic heart disease and stroke (Pega et al., 2021).

Many of us have been taken hostage by a worldview that values long hours focused on other people's business as a source to living a more fulfilled life, but there is clear evidence to counter that misconception. The findings from the aforementioned studies tell a contrary story of global proportions.

The following chart captures a recent data sampling of the extended work hours that have normalized globally for both self-employed and people working within other formalized organizational structures. Note that many people reflected in these numbers tend to be constituents of the working class or the poor within developing countries. Their extended hours of work reflect two primary conditions, 1) pushing against the trap of poverty that working only traditional work schedules would provide and 2) working to reflect the status of being "middle class" (as financially and socially defined within that nation's context of life and wealth). Just to give you a picture of what the fight for economic and social survival looks like from a global perspective, people who are regarded as middle class live on an average of $10.01–$20 a day. This is equates to yearly incomes between $14,600 and $29,200, not for singles but for a family of four (Kochhar, 2021).

Country	Average Number of Weekly Hours Worked
Bhutan	54.3
United Arab Emirates	52
Qatar	48.2
Lesotho	49.5
Qatar	48.2
Lebanon	48
Liberia	48
Republic of the Congo	47.9
Jordan	47
Pakistan	46.6
Brunei	46.6

* Chart reproduced from World Population Review based on November 2023 data projections and statical analysis tracking conducted by the International Labour Organization (ILO)

In comparison, other countries have a culture of work that in some cases is reduced by almost half. In the case of Europe: the *Netherlands, 26.7 hrs. a week; Norway, 27.1 hrs. a week; Vanuatu, 27.6 hrs. a week; Finland, 28.9 hrs. a week; Sweden, 29.2 hrs. a week.* Within the continent of Africa, nations like *Mozambique average 29.4 hrs.* of work a week. While a few nations in the Middle East, *Syria,* and *Yemen,* average a work culture of *25.3 hrs.* and *25.4 hrs. a week*, respectively (World Population Review, 2020; 2023). Clearly, there are huge discrepancies in values, globally, about how we work.

WHY THESE FACTS MATTER

The risk of being overworked is a risk anyone and everyone will face. From airline pilots to zoologists. From art therapists to Zumba instructors. With the number of hours worked nationally and internationally continuing to climb, there is less time left for the other key dimensions of your life—family and friends, accomplishing personal and learning goals, and investing in your mental and physical health. Life is more than work. It is marriage, it is dating (people and yourself). It's going back to school to complete that degree. It's spending more time with your children so that you can be a memorable part of their stages of development and celebrate their accomplishments. It's investing in yourself so that you can be of more value to the world in ways you often talk about but haven't yet gotten the time to do.

When we overwork and over-invest in what other people value and under-invest in what we value, we also narrow our capacity to be physically and emotionally available when and where it matters most. We are less likely to say yes to an unexpected invitation when we are overworked and overinvested. Less likely to say yes to an unexpected invitation to a play or concert, dinner with friends, or courtside season tickets that suddenly became available. Overinvesting in other people's priorities reduces the time you have for that workout at the gym, your commitment to the gardening club, your preparation for that bodybuilding competition next Spring, or that new language you've been wanting to learn. It even keeps you distracted from being fully emotionally present on birthdays, holidays, and the eternal moments when a loved one is transitioning from this life to the next.

With twenty-four hours (24) hours in a day and the increased work schedules as the relentless normal in many parts of the world, too many pivotal life-giving moments are slipping from our hands. It does not have to be this way. When we take back command of our time, we supercharge our creative energy and become equipped to deliver with precision when conditions call for it. Whether it be a three-week album deadline, as André 3000 did in the story I shared earlier, or any of those unexpected events that demand the gift of our attention, we can find joy in time rather than be mastered by time. We can take back our time and our lives and cultivate the momentum that transforms us forever.

4

✧ ✧ ✧ ✧ ✧ ✧ ✧ ✧ ✧ ✧ ✧

MOMENTUM REDEFINED

The word momentum is, without question, a word rich with good intentions. The mere use of the word inspires hope, optimism, and the belief that something can change for good. However, good intentions aren't enough. Intentions must accompany a decisive course of action guided by clear, hope-filled outcomes that can substantially influence our lives for good. *Remember, the job of momentum is to provide you with the series of thoughts and actions that keep you moving in the desired direction.*

The world's current understanding of momentum has good bones but it lacks the heft the more scientific meaning the term was meant to convey and that is, "momentum is intended not just to create movement but to add compounding value." Oversimplified definitions of the term have included:

→ "the force that keeps an object moving." (Cambridge Dictionary, 2024)
→ "the quality that keeps an event developing or making progress after it has started." (Cambridge Dictionary, 2024)
→ "1. the impetus of a moving object 2. strength or force that keeps growing." (Collins Dictionary, 2024)

I believe its meaning could be better. I would expand the definition of the term just a bit this way: **Momentum**—*is the determination to identify your most important goals and consistently dedicate the time, emotions, and tangible resources necessary to propel your progress toward achieving them so that you can expand your capacity in helping others reach their own.* When defined and understood this way, momentum is no longer an abstract and optimistic idea. It becomes actionable, and we become accountable for results.

5

✧ ✧ ✧ ✧ ✧ ✧ ✧ ✧ ✧ ✧ ✧

WHY THE MOMENTUM LIST |
THE ORIGIN STORY

I discovered that what I wanted to get done for the day was getting hijacked by other things on a list that I created but seemingly had no control over. The more experiences I gained, the greater the demands in my life and the more discontented I became with accepting competition for my mind and time. In other words, I needed to accomplish the things on *my* To-Do List without feeling like I prioritized other people's needs over mine. This way of living became increasingly intolerable for my mental health, sense of purpose, and vision for the future.

"I discovered that what I wanted to get done for the day was getting hijacked by other things on a list that I created but seemingly had no control over."

The Momentum List comes out of a commitment to live a fuller, more intentional life where I can be of service to others and benefit myself. As someone who was once a people pleaser and often willing to take on roles and responsibilities other people would avoid, I developed a default mechanism to *underserve* my primary needs and *overserve* the needs of others. However, serving your needs and the needs of others doesn't have to be a battle to the death. One does not have to win over the other, which is a cognitive and emotional shift in our perspective on priorities. Like many of you, I want my focus to reflect the other valued "f words" that are key resources in my life: family, fun, faith, and flexibility; this is when I birthed the concept of the Momentum List.

"The Momentum List comes out of a commitment to live a fuller, more intentional life where I can be of service to others and benefit myself."

The Momentum List, like your To-Do List, is a visual model that complements the mental image of your goal—your mental model. A mental model is essentially a picture we create in our mind of how something should look or a process for how something should be done. We use mental models to inform and guide our actions so that they are executed the way we envision them—at least close to how we pictured them. A mental model can range from something as simple as a stay-at-home dad's steps to prepare tomorrow's dinner to a CEO figuring out all the problems her organization could face with a new product launch.

"Mental models protect and prepare us to execute what is most important within a window of time."

"You need a shift from the conceptual—the idea of the action in your head, to the concrete—a visual of the behavior you are determined to execute. You need a Momentum List."

In the military, soldiers operate from mental models all the time. These mental models are called IAs (Immediate Actions) or IADs (Immediate Action Drills). IAs/IADs are a series of pre-planned actions that people in the military perform in response to unforeseen events or unexpected occurrences. It could be how to exit quickly in an emergency, what to do in response to an explosion, and the strategic actions to take when faced with an air attack, active extreme shooter, extreme flood, or massive power outage. Firefighters create mental models for how they approach entry into a burning building. A high school principal creates a mental model for tackling a difficult conversation with a staff member. We create mental models every day for different areas of our lives. Mental models are a defensive and counter-offensive strategy to help us manage the competition for our time. Mental models protect and prepare us to execute what is most important within a window of time.

WHY WE NEED TO SEE IT TO BELIEVE IT

Most people who live busy lives aren't eidetikers—able to remember things in exact detail as if you can see them in your mind. Most of us cannot recall vivid images and sensory details for a prolonged period after seeing them. Even fewer people have a photographic memory—the ability to remember details of things like the number of pages of a text, numbers, or events in great detail with exact precision. As a result, writing, sketching, and imaging things down manually on paper or a digital platform is a need for most of us. We need visual models that can support our mental models and connect us to the actions we plan to take. Mental models prepare us to execute what is most important within a window of time, but visual models give us a strategy for when and how we'll get it done.

Still, no matter how great or clear our mental model might be, putting it on paper, into our smart devices, and in our calendars—be it for business or something personal, helps us keep the details of our priorities in plain sight. Writing them down with as much specificity as possible creates the visual model we need, so nothing is left to chance, even if some of it changes.

So, what's the major takeaway? I'm glad you asked. It's this: Mental models ignite your vision for the future, but visual models help you establish momentum for it. You need a shift from the conceptual—the idea of the action in your head, to the concrete—a visual of the behavior you are determined to execute. That is why you need a Momentum List.

6

"… gaining momentum will cost us something, and we'll need to prepare ourselves and others for it as honestly and lovingly as possible."

✧ ✕ ✧ ✕ ✧ ✕ ✧ ✕ ✧ ✕ ✧

MOMENTUM COSTS

A To-Do List focuses on what matters to everyone else, while a Momentum List focuses on what matters to *you*. LeBron James, one of the greatest athletes in modern history, knows a little about building momentum. When asked, "What are three qualities that make a great basketball player?" sandwiched between "knowing the history of the game" and the "love of the game" was DISCIPLINE. He described it this way—

"Discipline. When it comes to discipline, you must sacrifice loved ones for a long time if you want to be great. It

is very unfortunate, and you feel it at times. You know the saying, "If it's too hot, get out of the kitchen?". Sometimes, you gotta get out of the kitchen because it gets hot. But you have to have the discipline to sometimes sacrifice loved ones to be great because they don't understand, and that's okay because they don't understand what it means to, like, I'm getting up every day at 5 or 6 a.m. When I get home after everyone leaves the gym, I'm going to take a nap. So now you're sacrificing your loved ones because you're not spending time with them, and when I wake up, I will probably train again. Then I'm going to have dinner, and then I'm going to bed, and I'm going to do that every single day for a long period of time. That's sacrifice and discipline."

(Mind of the Game Podcast, with Lebron James
and JJ Redick, 2024)

Lebron James' words may sound extreme. They may even produce a visceral reaction that makes you uncomfortable. However, he has exceptional quantifiable results proving that you can make that cost count if you plan. The challenge is that the human consciousness enjoys the pleasure of winning but not at a steep price. Many people want to earn a promotion at work but aren't willing to go the extra mile to make contributions outside of their job descriptions (and that does not have to mean working longer hours). Some people want to enjoy big payoffs and praise while avoiding problems and

"A To-Do List focuses on what matters to everyone else, while a Momentum List focuses on what matters to you."

pain. So, whether his words inspire or irritate you, we can't escape the essential truth behind Lebron's message—gaining momentum will cost us something, and we'll need to prepare ourselves and others for it as honestly and lovingly as possible.

GETTING OWNED BY OTHER PEOPLE'S PRIORITIES

Being a co-champion of other people's priorities and goals can be rewarding. Being at their mercy, not so much. Just imagine starting every day with what was important to everyone else but neglecting yourself, as Erica found herself in this scenario.

Erica's Impossible Exit. First thing in the morning, her alarm goes off. She wakes up and picks up her phone to check her email for new messages. A series of emails from a team member she leads marked "Priority" immediately catches her attention. After reading the email, Erica determines that she needs to take immediate action because she's convinced herself the fallout will negatively impact other team members and work streams if she doesn't. So, rather than grabbing her Bible, and heading to the kitchen to brew coffee, in her 30 minutes of quiet time before hitting the gym, she responds to emails. As Erica responds, she finds herself going down a rabbit hole of other tasks. She starts looking for the files her team member should already have access to but notes he can't find them and desperately needs help solving his current dilemma. As Erica wrestles through files on her laptop and moves items into a folder to share with him, she realizes that three other team members need the same support. So, what does she do? She starts to prep the files they'll need. By this time, her pre-planned 30 minutes of quiet time have come and gone and she's missed her morning workout, which she typically completes before the kids get up for school.

In a moment of unexpected self-loathing and disappointment, Erica looks up and thinks, "What just happened? Where did the time go?" Erica has just allowed someone else's needs to take her hostage. Her obsession with getting things right and being another person's problem solver has sent the start of her day in an entirely different direction. Instead of sticking with the few energizing priorities, she valued most that help her set the stage for the rest of the day— her quiet time, the simple pleasure of a freshly brewed cup of coffee before her kids awake, and her much-enjoyed workout, her plans are hijacked and her momentum subverted. Erica wants an AM do-over, but that ship has sailed. The time she hoped to invest in herself through a few life-giving actions that would better position her to serve others with joy and enthusiasm gets undermined, all because she allowed what could have been the small wins of her day to be outwitted by someone else's woes.

WHEN LIFE IS "LIFE-ING", YOU CAN'T DODGE IT!

Life will always be life-ing. In other words, you can always expect an unanticipated change, a new demand, and an unexpected emerging reality to turn life on its head. A new baby is born or enters the family. A new project gets added to your portfolio at work. A once independent family member suddenly needs more of your care. Each of these life experiences is important, demands your time, and costs you cognitive energy. However, none of them will take away the gnawing desire to spend time doing the key things that light a fire in your soul and help you feel ready to take on the day. Sure, your ego demands productivity to satiate its preferences. A way to measure your worth by the number of items you cross off as "Completed Tasks". However, your soul prefers momentum—a steady flow of energy and creativity nurtured not merely by getting things done but by engaging in the few critical habits of the day that create cognitive and emotional support systems. To-Do Lists are things you have to do. Momentum Lists are the things you can't live without doing. They are your soul food.

"To Do Lists are things you have to do. Momentum Lists are the things you can't live without doing."

7

✧ ✕ ✧ ✕ ✧ ✕ ✧ ✕ ✧ ✕ ✧

KNOW THE DIFFERENCE | THE TO-DO LIST VS. THE MOMENTUM LIST

To-Do lists typically consist of tasks that need to be completed—things that require attention in your personal, home, and work life. They can run the gamut of the things we "need to do," are "asked to do," and have "been directed to do." As you might tell, I'm no stranger to To-Do lists. After all, I am writing a book about them. I like them. I rely on To-Do Lists because I often have multiple things running through my mind that I intend to accomplish within a given day, week, or even month, and they need to be given a voice somewhere other than my head.

While To-Do Lists give my mind the space, it needs to articulate what it's thinking; a To-Do List can also be deceptively devaluing of your time and energy if it's only grounded in what you should do and need to do but is absent of what delights you. To-do lists are great at making demands on your time, which can, over time, be tremendously debilitating. A Momentum List supports the ways you can find delight in time.

Activities like dropping the kids at school or walking the dog before jumping into work, even grocery shopping and picking up your spouse from the airport, are often the kind of tasks and activities we do out of an obligation to others. These things are part of your To-Do List. However, things that help you maintain the right mindset and attitude to get the most out of your day—those actions that get you to delight in time, are likely different. Those habits and actions could include going for your morning run or swim, watering your plants, sipping a cup of freshly brewed coffee, or writing the third chapter of that new book. Maybe for you, it's getting up early to watch the sunrise, get in your first 40 ounces of water, and edit the latest episode of the podcast you plan to release at the end of the week. These simple yet meaningful actions go on your Momentum List. Why? These actions are accelerators for you. They are soul igniters. They set you up for success for the day and beyond because you have fed those areas that matter most. You have allowed yourself to experience a few early wins on your terms that will help to build sustained belief in yourself and what's possible.

"A Momentum List supports the ways you can find delight in time."

For example, I could, like Erica, get up earlier in the morning to respond to the overwhelming number of emails I receive daily, but that would compromise the time I've dedicated to working on this book, which will benefit not only my family but all the people this resource is intended to serve. The former would feed my ego and the desire to see other people have their needs met, but circumvent the latter more foundational need to feed my own soul and set me up for a healthy outlook on the day which in turn would enable me to also serve others' needs more effectively. Both checking emails and writing this book are important and make demands on my time, but the latter—writing this book, offers the added value of helping me find delight in how I use time; it shifts my outlook, not merely my outcome.

YOUR ROADMAP TO MOMENTUM |
KEY CRITERIA OF A MOMENTUM LIST

Our Momentum List—those 2-3 actionable investments of time that set the tone for our day, are often buried in our To-Do lists but need to be lifted to the surface as the few priorities we can leverage for establishing our momentum. There are moments when our lives are so off track and mis-prioritized that the investment of time committed to feeding our momentum can seem distant and unreachable, but that's still no reason to give up on reclaiming that momentum and giving those small investments their rightful place.

"Since what it takes to forge momentum in your life will be unique to you, every- one's Momentum List will not look the same."

Your Momentum List should be limited to the few actions or habits that can fertilize the soil of your time, creativity, and vision for the day, week, and even beyond. The activities and priorities on your Momentum List pay dividends to your future mentally, physically, relationally, and directly or indirectly. They are the matches that ignite a deep commitment and concentration on the other aspects of your life that also demand your attention—the people, processes, and places on your more expansive list of demands. Since what it takes to forge momentum in your life will be unique to you, everyone's Momentum List will not look the same. Nor will it remain the same forever since you and I are ever-evolving people. However, every Momentum List will always need to meet specific clear criteria for you to gain traction toward what you most value. When it comes to cultivating momentum and identifying what should be on your Momentum List consider the following criteria:

→ Includes 2–3 "life-giving" specific and actionable items that set the tone for your day.
→ Helps you achieve early wins that ignite your focus, vision, and creativity for the present and the future.
→ Supports how you find delight in time rather than being mastered by it.
→ Allows you to serve yourself well first so you can be more effective at serving others.

Creating a Momentum List sounds relatively simple, so why

do we struggle to prioritize the crucial tasks that shape our day and pave the way for early victories that yield significant benefits in other areas of our lives? I would argue that it has more to do with how we think—our mindset—than what we do.

8

"Often, the things we care about the most don't get our first attention because, at the core, most people are people-pleasers."

❖ ❖ ❖ ❖ ❖ ❖ ❖ ❖ ❖ ❖ ❖

WHY WE STRUGGLE TO
OWN OUR MOMENTUM

Navigating between our priorities and external expectations is a challenge. Often, the things we care about the most don't get our first attention because, at the core, most people are people-pleasers. In 2022, YouGov, a British international internet-based marketing research and data analytics firm, surveyed 1,000 adults in the United States. The results indicated that nearly half (49%) of the respondents identified themselves as people-pleasers, with 60% expressing that being a people-pleaser came naturally to them (YouGov, 2022). Of the people surveyed, it was noted that two-thirds of them, 70% of whom identified as women and 63% as men said they go to great lengths to avoid conflict. Another interesting finding from this poll was the number of people who agreed they "Put other people's needs first, at the expense of their own" (YouGov, 2022) 68% of women and 64% of men noted they do it somewhat often or very often. Pretty significant? If this poll reflects society, we can see why it is so easy for people to focus on a To-Do List filled with other people's business instead of their Momentum List, which is all about their own business. Most people prefer minding other people's business more than their own or, at the very least, they have been conditioned to.

Don't get me wrong, caring for others is essential and can be a life-giving activity when not done at the expense of tending to your soul's need to be invested in and loved. Prioritizing caring for others over yourself as an unboundaried habit fosters resentment, and eventually hinders your ability to serve others well. It is akin to helping others put on their life vest but refusing to put on your own. It is a sure way to watch everyone else make it safely to shore during an emergency while you get overtaken by the waves, pulled under by the current, and drown.

On a plane, the crew guides passengers through what to do in an emergency before take-off. The safety directions provided by Delta Airlines are an example of how important it is to set the stage in gaining momentum for yourself so you can then effectively support the priorities of everyone else—

"It's unlikely but if cabin pressure changes oxygen masks will drop from the panels above your seat and inside the lavatories. Reach up and pull the mask or the streamer down to start the flow of oxygen. Remove any face covering and place the mask over your nose and mouth, slip the elastic strap over your head, and adjust the mask, if necessary. Breathe normally and note the oxygen is flowing, so you don't have to worry if the bag doesn't inflate. Be sure to adjust your mask before helping others ... "

(Delta Airline, Delta Airlines Safety Video, 2023)

Your Momentum List is your oxygen, and its job is to support the life-sustaining experiences of your day that you cannot afford to neglect.

9

"Be sure to adjust your own mask before helping others." —Delta Airlines

✧ ✧ ✧ ✧ ✧ ✧ ✧ ✧ ✧ ✧ ✧ ✧

YOUR MOMENTUM,
AN ACT OF GENEROSITY TO OTHERS

Generosity in any direction requires the *heart* (the will to do it), *mind* (a specific motivation for it), and *time* (the availability to make it happen). When you discipline your mind, emotions, and behavior to add momentum to your daily fuel tank first before you commit to supporting everyone else's goals and objectives, you execute in service to others with joy rather than resentment. You have done what the Delta Airlines safety directions advised: " . . . adjust(ed) your own mask before helping others . . . "

So, when you think about it, our ability to open the door of our heart and mind and pockets generously toward other priorities requires us to clear our mental and emotional pallet of the unfinished actions our brains value most. When we complete the most critical tasks, we free our minds and emotions to focus on other outstanding tasks generously. When we do not complete the most essential tasks, our brains will not let us get away with them. It is the result of something called the *Zeigarnik Effect*. Named after Russian psychiatrist and psychologist Bluma Wulfovna Zeigarnik, the Zeigarnik Effect happens when the ongoing pressure of leaving something important undone keeps your brain from peacefully focusing on anything else until it is done. The Zeigarnik Effect asserts that people remember incomplete tasks even more than those they have completed (Zeigarnik, 1927; Burke, 2011). We will not forget that task until it is finished.

People who know the benefit of doing the few key things each day that help them establish momentum for their lives and implement them regularly are the most effective in meeting the needs of others because they have committed to living a life that reflects their values. People who live in alignment with their values experience decreased cognitive dissonance. They experience immediate wins with the 2–3 three priorities that produce momentum in their lives, which promotes positive emotional well-being and liberates the cognitive capital needed to invest their time, energy, and emotions in the areas that need their deep focus and attention.

"People who know the benefit of doing the few key things each day that help them establish momentum for their lives and implement them regularly are the most effective … because they have committed to living a life that reflects their values."

DRAWING THE HEAT OF YOUR FOCUS IN THE RIGHT DIRECTION

The heat of your focus needs to be pulled in the right direction to get the most out of what you expect that focus to yield. It is comparable to turning on an exhaust fan above the stove in your kitchen. What's cooking in the pan are the 2–3 life-giving actions you do that help to create the momentum for your day. As you accomplish them, the energy—the steam, smoke, and heat produced by each of those items gets absorbed in the list of small wins for the day that you get to check off as done. At the same time, the oxygen in the room isn't thick with the smoke of your Momentum List left undone and can handle you putting a few more pots on the stove to get the things on your To-Do List cooking and in motion. In essence, you can now give time, space, and resources in other areas for the benefit of others. The feeling of competing for how you use your own time is less prevalent. You are emotionally and cognitively free to give of yourself without overwhelming impatience and resentment because you invested in the life-giving tasks—your Momentum List. You can now delight in time rather than be mastered by it because you served yourself well first. What matters to you most for the day was done, and now the critical needs of people, places, and projects, reflected on your To-Do list, can get the care they need.

I find little joy and gratitude in serving others each day if I've short-changed myself in making focused investments in some of the critical priorities that set my momentum for the day. On most days, my Momentum List includes:

→ Morning workout (a multi-mile hike or intense cardio and weightlifting fitness routine)
→ Devotional time—pray, read scripture, and listen to God
→ Enjoying my morning coffee while I review and respond to emails

On other days, my Momentum List looks different based on what I know intuitively and on the longer-term goals towards which I need to make traction. It could look like this:

→ Devotional time—pray, read scripture, and listen to God
→ Do a load of laundry for the family for our upcoming trip
→ Record upcoming episodes for my podcast

When I engage my day with the behaviors my head and heart value most *first*, listening to and tending to the needs of others feels more like a privilege than a burden. I'm increasingly more agile, attentive, and patient with people and processes. There may be something to be said about the Zeigarnik Effect after all!

10

❖❖❖❖❖❖❖❖❖❖❖

PERSONALIZING MOMENTUM |
EMBRACING YOUR DISTINCT NEEDS

You have unique life circumstances, responsibilities, needs, and vision. Maybe it's:

→ Spending 60 minutes at the top of your day writing the manuscript for the screenplay or book you want to publish
→ Completing a 40-minute HIIT (high-intensity interval training) routine before working the night shift
→ Ensuring the kids' lunches are made and packed

OR

- → Reviewing the schedule for the upcoming day to edit events and actions where necessary
- → Checking your child's homework before you go to bed to make sure it is complete and his/her best work.
- → Directing your kids to pick out and iron their clothes for the next day so you can sleep well and reduce the need to rush in the morning, which creates its own set of anxieties

Each person's Momentum List is different, but every Momentum List shares the same actions to set you up for success in what's ahead and fits the criteria of:

- → 2–3 "life-giving" specific and actionable items that set the tone for your day.
- → Helping you achieve early wins that ignite your focus, vision, and creativity for the present and the future.
- → Supporting how you find delight in time rather than being mastered by it.
- → Allows you to serve yourself well first so you can be more effective at serving others.

11

✧ ✕ ✧ ✕ ✧ ✕ ✧ ✕ ✧ ✕

LET'S GET TACTICAL

Let's be honest. In reality, on any given day, you might be overwhelmed with so much to do that taking the time to stop, evaluate, and get particular about what is on your To-Do List(s) feels like a lost cause or a waste of time; this is a fair and "perfectly" normal reaction. However, I promise you . . . it won't be. Remember the Delta Airlines safety guidelines? Now ask yourself the question—" If I were on a plane that needed to make an emergency landing and the oxygen masks dropped from the panels above my seat, would I be better prepared to help other people before or after I got the flow of oxygen in motion in my lungs?

Your ability to joyfully help other people get "oxygen" released into their lungs (the priorities of their day, week, month, and even beyond) is contingent upon securing the oxygen flow to your own. Do you get the metaphor? You can no longer avoid investing the relatively short period it will take to step back and examine what you have been giving your time to and how you have been overserving others and undeserving yourself. The risk of creating a hostile environment is no longer worth it.

UNCOVERING YOUR PATH TO MOMENTUM

Here is a simple approach to quickly combing through your To-Do List to identify what belongs on your Momentum List. You'll want to **Sketch/Script it** (draft your priorities), **Scrutinize it** (determine which priorities are "fire for the future"—the small wins that ignite your focus, vision, and creativity that will inevitably benefit you and as a by product, others), **Stamp it** (Label with an M, circle, or highlight the priorities). **Scale it** (move those life-giving actions to the top of the list and execute with consistency).

SKETCH/SCRIPT IT

First, draft or review your To-Do List for the week. If you are not in the habit of producing momentum for the things that matter most to you, your list will likely be indiscriminate and include your and other people's priorities.

SCRUTINIZE IT

Next, ask yourself, "What on this list motivates, energizes, and sets me up for getting the most out of my day and even the week ahead?"

→ You should feel an emotional connection to each item on the list because they ignite your focus, vision, and creativity for the present and future. Once accomplished, these actions make serving everyone else's needs a pleasure rather than a pain.

→ They should be actionable and provide you with early wins. If you spend time on these, you'll be able to tackle the other items with a lot more energy and enthusiasm.

STAMP IT

Then, you'll want to stamp it. Label those 2–3 "life-giving" actions on that list with an **M** for Momentum. You can even circle or highlight the priorities. It's your choice but make them stand out.

SCALE IT

Elevate these items and actions to the top of your list. They represent your essential priorities—the fuel for channeling your energy, passion, and focus to maximize personal performance and contribute effectively to others. This is your Momentum List. Now, move those life-giving actions to the top of the list and execute with consistency.

SKETCH/SCRIPT IT. SCRUTINIZE IT. STAMP IT.
SCALE IT.

For me, there are typically 1 to 3 things on the list of 10 or 20 items that get the *Stamp* from me. I then block off a segment of time to commit to those items. Even if I don't get all of it done, I invest enough energy into the activities on my Momentum List so that the appetite for doing more of it later brings me back the next day. Each time I execute on my Momentum List, I'm creating a pattern. I'm developing the habit of focusing on what I deem a priority, an investment in myself that I know, once accomplished, will free me emotionally and cognitively to give my best in the areas I'm needed and counted on without the regret of having left myself for last.

BECOME A SKILLED SCALER

As you scale it, your practice of investing in your Momentum List becomes almost intuitive because you have built the muscle memory to own what you value most. This way, when life throws curveballs and priorities shift, you can recalibrate and identify what will drive your momentum during that phase. Having practiced prioritizing yourself—motivated not by selfishness but by the desire to accomplish and invest in what truly matters—you'll be well-prepared to prioritize effectively and handle other responsibilities with care.

12

✧✵✧✵✧✵✧✵✧✵✧

In the following section, we've compiled a handful of visual models of the process for developing your Momentum List. While all of these visual models follow the **Sketch/ Script it—Scrutinize it—Stamp it—Scale it Protocol**, we deliberately called out the specific strategy—*Sketching/ Scripting, Scrutinizing, or Stamping*, each person used as a primary driver for identifying the 2–3 "life-giving" specific and actionable items that aligned with the criteria of a Momentum List. We recommend using these as guides to help you create mental and visual models for designing your Momentum List. You will find that the better you scale your Momentum List, the more intuitive you get at executing them, even if those drivers of momentum change over time. You will delight in using the time your Momentum List provides to support others counting on you.

REMEMBER THE MOMENTUM LIST CRITERIA . . .

→ Includes 2–3 "life-giving" specific and actionable items that set the tone for your day.

→ Helps you achieve early wins that ignite your focus, vision, and creativity for the present and the future.

→ Supports how you find delight in time rather than being mastered by it.

→ Allows you to serve yourself well first so you can be more effective at serving others.

Moment*um* Model One

KIAAN, a millennial CEO of a tech company in India, reassesses his values by scrutinizing the ten most common actions on his almost daily To-Do List and uncovers three (3) specific and actionable items that will help him achieve early wins for the day. Scaling these early wins will ignite his focus, vision, and creativity to lead his company enthusiastically. Kiaan's commitment to reorienting what mattered to him most helped him not only find delight in time but also caused him to make the remaining priorities sequential moves of his day that added momentum.

To-Do-*List*

Schedule a 15-minute virtual coffee meeting with the new department head to foster collaboration and understand team dynamics.

Spend 30 minutes reviewing and updating the quarterly business strategy.

Spend 30 minutes reading industry news and staying updated on tech trends.

Identify one actionable improvement based on customer insights to implement immediately.

Attend strength conditioning class to support practice rounds with the Cricket team.

Evaluate cash flow projections and financial performance metrics and schedule feedback meetings with the CFO.

Review team outputs and recognize outstanding team member achievements during weekly meetings.

Water plants in the garden before dawn.

Allocate time to participate in 3 of the 5 community or industry-related events this week and coordinate schedule changes that will support that shift.

Review tech executive pipeline training modules to prep for the weekly online course and the two weekly public interest technology workgroups I'm facilitating.

Momentum *List*

Water plants in the garden before dawn.

Review tech executive pipeline training modules to prepare for the weekly online course and the two weekly public interest technology workgroups I'm facilitating.

Attend strength conditioning class to support practice rounds with the Cricket team.

Spend 30 minutes reading industry news and staying updated on tech trends.

Spend 30 minutes reviewing and updating the quarterly business strategy.

Identify one actionable improvement based on customer insights to implement immediately.

Review team outputs and recognize outstanding team member achievements during weekly meetings.

Conduct a 15-minute virtual coffee meeting with the new department head each morning to foster collaboration and understand team dynamics.

Evaluate cash flow projections and financial performance metrics and schedule feedback meetings with the CFO.

Allocate time to participate in 3 of the 5 community or industry-related events this week and coordinate schedule changes that will support that shift.

Moment*um* Model Two

KELIS, a working mother of four (4) and the lead project manager for an engineering firm has been living through a pretty hectic season. Her efforts to refocus her energy toward the mindset and actions that are non-negotiable so she can witness progress in her own life while she excels in her industry led to a shift in her priorities to ensure that she finds delight in time rather than being mastered by it. **Scrutinizing** her To-Do List showed her that one of the items she thought was a priority did not belong within her scope of focus so she removed it. She is now able to identify ways to get her children connected to the people and experiences that will help address some of the social and emotional needs that have surfaced over the past few months.

To-Do-*List*

Prepare and enjoy a healthy breakfast with the kids to start the day positively. −M

~~Set aside dedicated blocks of time for work tasks, errands, and quality time with children.~~

Break down the two project plans for the engineering team into smaller tasks and prioritize them based on the deadlines we discussed.

Complete a 50-minute morning yoga or Pilates session daily −M

Check and respond to urgent work emails or messages before noon.

Plan the weekly support group for working single mothers.

Dedicate an hour to my online project management training course (positions me to meet my financial goals). −M

Review and update the family budget on the financial planning App.

Delegate two age-appropriate chores to Derrick and Clinton so they learn how to help with household tasks.

Momentum *List*

Complete a 50-minute morning yoga or Pilates session daily.

Prepare and enjoy a healthy breakfast with the kids to start the day positively.

Dedicate an hour to my online project management training course (positions me to meet my financial goals).

Break down the two project plans for the engineering team into smaller tasks and prioritize them based on the deadlines we discussed.

Check and respond to urgent work emails or messages before noon.

Review and update the family budget on the financial planning App.

Plan the weekly support group for working single mothers.

Delegate two age-appropriate chores to Derrick and Clinton so they learn how to help with household tasks.

Momentum Model Three

DOMINIC, a divorced father of 2 who is a surgeon in a large metropolitan hospital, rediscovered the two (2) priorities he needed to resurface but that he had allowed his accessibility to other people's needs to hijack. Stamping these two priorities and moving them up on his Momentum List set the tone for his day and enabled him to find delight in time rather than being mastered by it. Making the time to pause and step away from living on autopilot allowed him to create a new visual model for his day. He now realizes that a morning ritual of taking care of his family relationships, physical well-being, and plans of care for his patients could co-exist rather than compete with each other if he is intentional about making it happen.

To-Do-*List*	Momentum *List*
Create a detailed schedule for surgeries and patient consultations, prioritizing urgent cases.	**Send an "I love you" text to the girls.**
Delegate administrative tasks to support staff to streamline workflow and reduce stress levels.	**Go for a morning run before my second shift.**
Collaborate with the medical review board to develop the professional development series for the coming year.	**Enjoy a healthy breakfast while reviewing the day's surgical cases and patient charts.**
Send an "I love you" text to the girls.	Dedicate 20 minutes to reading medical journals or researching advancements in surgical techniques.
Go for a morning run before my second shift.	Delegate administrative tasks to support staff to streamline workflow and reduce stress levels.
Dedicate 20 minutes to reading medical journals or researching advancements in surgical techniques.	Create a detailed schedule for surgeries and patient consultations, prioritizing urgent cases.
Conduct morning rounds to check patient progress and update medical records.	Collaborate with the medical review board to develop the professional development series for the coming year.
Enjoy a healthy breakfast while reviewing the day's surgical cases and patient charts.	Outline the supply list for the camping trip with the girls and reserve the RV.
Outline the supply list for the camping trip with the girls and reserve the RV.	Conduct morning rounds to check patient progress and update medical records.

Moment*um* Model Four

TRACEY, is a 20-year-old college student with a demanding sociology course schedule who has identified three priorities that set the tone for her day. This Momentum List will help Tracey experience early wins and delight in time rather than being mastered by it. While Tracey has always been conscientious about her priorities, going through this process helped her reflect on why her A.M. weightlifting routine is such a linchpin in her day. It fed her need for community. Tracey realized that when she starts her day doing something she loves with a small community, she is more likely to use the time she invested in the other obligations on her list to build relationships – from the study group with classmates to coaching the youth league and keeping the dorm in excellent living condition with her suitemates. Reordering her List and placing the few things that create momentum at the top of her day allowed her to invest in serving herself well first to be even better at serving others.

To-Do-*List*

Wake up at 5:30 a.m. and get in a 90-minute weightlifting session with the guys at the campus gym.

Finish assigned reading for today's classes and prep for the study group.

Attend classes.

Spend an hour on the Qualitative Research course proposal for my senior thesis.

Proof and print sociology paper.

Volunteer to coach the youth basketball league.

Grab breakfast with Eddie and Mo at the student union building.

Clean dorm suite.

Momentum *List*

Wake up at 5:30 a.m. and get in a 90-minute weightlifting session with the guys at the campus gym.

Spend an hour on the Qualitative Research course proposal for my senior thesis.

Grab breakfast with Eddie and Mo at the student union building.

Finish assigned reading for today's classes and prep for the study group.

Attend classes.

Volunteer to coach the youth basketball league.

Proof and print sociology paper.

Clean dorm suite.

Appendices

✧ ✧ ✧ ✧ ✧ ✧ ✧ ✧ ✧ ✧ ✧

GIVE IT A SHOT |
OWNING YOUR MOMENTUM

In the following pages—the Appendices, you'll have the space to practice resetting the priorities that establish the momentum you need to make the most significant impact on your day. This will be an opportunity for you to create a visual model for what matters most in your life as you bring those habits and actions back to the top—of your list and your life.

You'll Need:

→ Your current list of priorities—personal and

professional.

→ The Momentum List Criteria: You will reference it as you decide which priorities to elevate and which to demote from your existing list.

→ Use the **Sketch/Script it–Scrutinize it–Stamp it–Scale it Protocol** to help you reflect on and reform the list of priorities.

→ 15–30 minutes of uninterrupted time (depending on how long your list might be) to move your mental model of the new way you want to leverage your time and energy to a visual model you can own and execute.

I added the criteria for the *Momentum List and* the steps for the Sketch/Script it–Scrutinize it–Stamp it–Scale it protocol at the top of each page to keep you from having to move back and forth between pages. Feel free to use the charts provided to build your Momentum List or the blank pages behind them to re-envision your priorities. You know what works best for you.

THE PEN, THE HEAD, AND THE HEART

For many of us, technology is the primary driver in how we create and communicate. I get it; it is for me as well! I leverage everything my smartphone has to offer—including the notepad to document notes and ideas, and the voice recorder to save audio memos that capture the nuances of things I need to remember. Even task reminders on my network applications for work are saved on my phone.

However, something magical happens when I put pen to paper, even for just a few minutes. My preliminary thoughts become clearer and more concrete when I put pen to paper—that's important for the worlds I'm responsible for managing—from my personal to my professional life.

That being said, I encourage you to let the power of the pen or pencil work for you in this process. Research and science continue to confirm that when we put our hands to pen and paper, the brain becomes deeply engaged in the task.

So if you are serious about establishing momentum in your life, leverage the pen before technology to stimulate the engagement of your head and your heart.

DON'T FRET, A DIGITAL VERSION IS ON THE WAY

If you're a techie, rest assured. I have your back. While the visual models here encourage you to consider a pen (or pencil) drafting method for reimagining your To-Do List to create your life-changing Momentum List, a digital version of the framework will soon be available. You will be able to sketch/script your Momentum List. Save it, share it, and even make it accessible to key people who need to be kept in step with how you have committed to reshaping your life. Visit stephenvpeters.com for updates.

Now back to building your momentum!

Practice Moment*um* Model One

Includes 2-3 "life-giving" specific and actionable items that set the tone for your day.

Helps you achieve early wins that ignite your focus, vision, and creativity for the present and the future.

Supports how you find delight in time rather than being mastered by it.

Allows you to serve yourself well first so you can be more effective at serving others.

Sketch *it*/Script *it*
Draft your priorities

Scrutinize *it*
Determine which priorities are "fire for the future" – the small wins that ignite your focus, vision, and creativity that will inevitably benefit you and, as a product, others

Stamp *it*
Label with an M, circle, or highlight the priorities

Scale *it*
Move those life-giving actions to the top of the list and execute with consistency

MANAGING DEMANDS ON MY TIME **VS.** DELIGHT IN MY TIME

To-Do-*List*

Momentum *List*

Practice Moment*um* Model Two

Includes 2-3 "life-giving" specific and actionable items that set the tone for your day.

Helps you achieve early wins that ignite your focus, vision, and creativity for the present and the future.

Supports how you find delight in time rather than being mastered by it.

Allows you to serve yourself well first so you can be more effective at serving others.

Sketch *it*/Script *it*

Draft your priorities

Scrutinize *it*

Determine which priorities are "fire for the future" – the small wins that ignite your focus, vision, and creativity that will inevitably benefit you and, as a product, others

Stamp *it*

Label with an M, circle, or highlight the priorities

Scale *it*

Move those life-giving actions to the top of the list and execute with consistency

MANAGING DEMANDS ON MY TIME **VS.** DELIGHT IN MY TIME

To-Do-*List*

Momentum *List*

Practice Moment*um* Model Three

Includes 2-3 "life-giving" specific and actionable items that set the tone for your day.

Helps you achieve early wins that ignite your focus, vision, and creativity for the present and the future.

Supports how you find delight in time rather than being mastered by it.

Allows you to serve yourself well first so you can be more effective at serving others.

Sketch *it*/Script *it*

Draft your priorities

Scrutinize *it*

Determine which priorities are "fire for the future" – the small wins that ignite your focus, vision, and creativity that will inevitably benefit you and, as a product, others

Stamp *it*

Label with an M, circle, or highlight the priorities

Scale *it*

Move those life-giving actions to the top of the list and execute with consistency

Practice Moment*um* Model Four

Includes 2-3 "life-giving" specific and actionable items that set the tone for your day.

Helps you achieve early wins that ignite your focus, vision, and creativity for the present and the future.

Supports how you find delight in time rather than being mastered by it.

Allows you to serve yourself well first so you can be more effective at serving others.

Sketch *it*/Script *it*
Draft your priorities

Scrutinize *it*
Determine which priorities are "fire for the future" – the small wins that ignite your focus, vision, and creativity that will inevitably benefit you and, as a product, others

Stamp *it*
Label with an M, circle, or highlight the priorities

Scale *it*
Move those life-giving actions to the top of the list and execute with consistency

Conclusion

❖❖❖❖❖❖❖❖❖❖

Now that you know what the Momentum List is all about and have had some time to practice developing your own, there are two long-term impacts of committing to a lifestyle driven not just by the plethora of things you have to do but by the shortlist of habits and actions you value most. The actions that create the conditions for all the other things in your life that matter. They are *personal integrity* and *legacy*. To cultivate your Momentum List and build it into your daily lifestyle communicates that you are determined to be someone who is a winner *and* a finisher. A winner because living by your Momentum List enables you to experience small wins daily and early. A finisher, because by nature of your small early wins each day, you build the muscle memory to finish what you start in connection to your own goals and objectives. You become someone who has the tenacity to follow through on what they believe, and that is a fundamental trait of personal integrity. Developing your Momentum List is a way of being honest and truthful about the values and principles for living that you want to shape your life. It is that level of honesty and commitment to your Momentum List that enables you to delight in time rather than be mastered by it; it's a joy that will be experienced by everyone your life touches.

When it comes to legacy, the Momentum List creates a framework and supports the mindset for the habits of living that, as you implement and stick with them will have ripple effects on the people in your life. Your Momentum List as you "own it" and implement it daily showcases a pattern of living that becomes a resource on how others can invest their time, will, and emotions in productive ways. Your Momentum List lifestyle becomes the source of retraining the lifelong habits of others in how they not only manage other people's business but how they take control of managing their own because they witness how you live this out.

My hope is that as you move forward and internalize this new approach to managing your life, you also cultivate the wisdom for knowing when it's time to step back and reassess when even your Momentum List needs to be recalibrated. When you do, you can re-prioritize your energies toward the shift of personal habits and practices that will be replaced as the igniting forces of your momentum so you can be even more impactful in supporting the needs, goals, and ambitions of others.

Bibliography

American Psychological Association. (2021). *The American workforce faces compounding pressure*. APA. Retrieved from—https://www.apa.org/pubs/reports/work-well-being/compounding-pressure-2021

Bernhardt, J., Recksiedler, C., & Linberg, A. (2022). Work from home and parenting: Examining the role of work–family conflict and gender during the COVID-19 pandemic. *Journal of Social Issues*. https://Doi.org/10.1111/josi.12509

Blackwell, R. J. (1966). Descartes' Laws of Motion. *Isis, 57*(2), 220–234. http://www.jstor.org/stable/227961

Bureau of Labor Statistics. (2023). *AMERICAN TIME USE SURVEY–2022 RESULTS*. https://www.bls.gov/news.release/pdf/atus.pdf

Burrows, M., Burd, C., & Mckenzie, B. (2023). *Home-Based*

Workers and the COVID-19 Pandemic American Community Survey Reports. https://www.census.gov/content/dam/Census/library/publications/2023/acs/acs-52.pd

Cambridge.(n.d.). Momentum. *In Cambridge.org dictionary.* Retrieved June 8, 2024, from https://dictionary.cambridge.org/us/dictionary/english/momentum.

Collins. (n.d.). Momentum. In Collins.com dictionary. Retrieved June 8, 2024, from https://www.collinsdictionary.com/us/dictionary/english/momentum.

Delta Airline (2023, February 1). Delta Airlines Safety Video | 2023. Retrieved from—https://www.youtube.com/watch?v=-G1eljc4ZTU&t=21s.

Fowler, Michael (n.d.) Momentum, Work, and Energy. Retrieved from—https://galileoandeinstein.phys.virginia.edu/lectures/momentum.html

Glen Science Center, NASA.Stanford Encyclopedia of Philosophy (*Fri Jul 29, 2005; substantive revision Fri Oct 15, 2021). Descartes' Physics. Retrieved from*—https://plato.stanford.edu/entries/descartes-physics/#SpacBodyMoti

Haan, K. (2023, June 12). *Remote Work Statistics & Trends In (2023)—Forbes Advisor.* www.forbes.com. https://www.forbes.com/advisor/business/remote-work-statistics/#sources_section

Infra-Annual Labor Statistics: Working-Age Population Total: From 25 to 54 Years for United States. (2024). Stlouisfed.org. https://fred.stlouisfed.org/series/LFWA25TTUSM647N

Iso-Ahola, S. E., & Dotson, C. O. (2016). Psychological Momentum—A Key to Continued Success. *Frontiers in Psychology*, *7*. https://doi.org/10.3389/fpsyg.2016.01328

Kochhar, R. (2021, July 21). Are you in the global middle class? Find out with our income calculator. Pew Research Center; Pew Research Center. https://www.pewresearch.org/short -reads/2021/07/21/are-you-in-the-global-middle-class-find -out-with-our-income-calculator/#:~:text=As%20our%20 study%20defines%20it

Mind of the Game. (2024, March 19). *What makes a great basketball player? | LeBron James & JJ Redick | Full episode. [Video].* YouTube. Retrieved from—https://www.youtube .com/watch?v=q2XVtWfancQ

NASA Glenn Research Center. (2024, June 27). *Newton's Laws of Motion | Glenn Research Center | NASA.* Glenn Research Center | NASA. Retrieved from—https://www1. grc.nasa.gov/beginners-guide-to-aeronautics/newtons- laws-of-motion/#:~:text=Newton's%20Third%20 Law%3A%20Action%20%26%20Reaction&text=His%20 third%20law%20states%20that,opposite%20 force%20on%20object%20A.

Newport, C. (2016). *Deep Work: Rules for Focused Success in a Distracted World*. Grand Central Publishing.

Organization for Economic Co-operation and Development. (2024, August 15). *Working Age Population: Aged 15–64: All Persons for the United States*. FRED, Federal Reserve Bank of St. Louis. https://fred.stlouisfed.org/series/LFWA64TTUSM647S.

Otonkorpi-Lehtoranta, K., Salin, M., Hakovirta, M., & Kaittila, A. (2021). Gendering boundary work: Experiences of work-family practices among Finnish working parents during COVID-19 lockdown. *Gender, Work & Organization*, *29*(6). https://doi.org/10.1111/gwao.12773

Ozimek, A. (2021). *Future Workforce Report 2021 | Upwork*. Www.upwork.com. https://www.upwork.com/research/future-workforce-report

Parker, K. (2023, March 30). *About a third of U.S. workers who can work from home now do so all the time*. Pew Research Center. https://www.pewresearch.org/short-reads/2023/03/30/about-a-third-of-us-workers-who-can-work-from-home-do-so-all-the-time/

Pega, F., Náfrádi, B., Momen, N. C., Ujita, Y., Streicher, K. N., Prüss-Üstün, A. M., Descatha, A., Driscoll, T., Fischer, F. M., Godderis, L., Kiiver, H. M., Li, J., Magnusson Hanson,

L. L., Rugulies, R., Sørensen, K., & Woodruff, T. J. (2021). *Global, regional, and national burdens of ischemic heart disease and stroke attributable to exposure to long working hours for 194 countries, 2000–2016: A systematic analysis from the WHO/ILO Joint Estimates of the Work-related Burden of Disease and Injury.* Environment International, 154(106595), 106595. https://doi.org/10.1016/j.envint.2021.106595

QLS Classic: LA Reid Part 3. (2024, April 29). Apple Podcasts. https://podcasts.apple.com/us/podcast/questlove-supreme/id1485250501?i=1000576323581

Stanford Encyclopedia of Philosophy (*Fri Jul 29, 2005; substantive revision Fri Oct 15, 2021). Descartes' Physics. Retrieved from—*https://plato.stanford.edu/entries/descartes-physics/#SpacBodyMoti

World Population Review. (2020; Updated 2023, November). *Average Work Week by Country 2020.* Worldpopulationreview.com. https://worldpopulationreview.com/country-rankings/average-work-week-by-country

Zeigarnik, B. (1927). On Finished and unfinished tasks. Retrieved from—https://www.codeblab.com/wp-content/uploads/2009/12/On-Finished-and-Unfinished-Tasks.pdf.

About the Author

Dr. Stephen V. Peters is a missional leader, speaker, and educator with expertise in leadership coaching and conflict resolution. As the host of the **Take Care & Live!**™ podcast, he is passionately dedicated to human development, helping individuals thrive at the intersections of life. Stephen has successfully led large teams and organizations in both public education and nonprofit sectors, navigating complex challenges and driving innovation.

As a social scientist, his research explores the impact of fathers on their children's educational journeys and delves into gender and leadership—work that has garnered national and international recognition.

Outside of coaching, writing, and podcasting, Stephen enjoys hiking, traveling with his talented wife, April, nurturing his family, and fostering community connections.

To learn more, visit www.stephenvpeters.com and connect with him on social media for access to new and upcoming publications and content.